GUN CONTROL

Is It a Right or a Danger to Bear Arms?

Steve Otfinoski

Twenty-First Century Books

A Division of Henry Holt and Company
New York

Twenty-First Century Books
A division of Henry Holt and Company, Inc.
115 West 18th Street
New York, New York 10011

Henry Holt® and colophon are registered trademarks of Henry Holt and Company, Inc.
Publishers since 1866

Published in Canada by Fitzhenry & Whiteside Ltd.
91 Granton Drive, Richmond Hill, Ontario L4B 2N5

Printed in Mexico

Created and produced in association with Blackbirch Graphics, Inc.

Library of Congress Cataloging-in-Publication Data

Otfinoski, Steven.
    Gun control: is it a right or a danger to bear arms? / Steven Otfinoski — 1st ed.
        p.   cm. — (Issues of our time)
    Published in Canada by Fitzhenry & Whiteside Ltd.
    Includes bibliographical references and index.
    ISBN 0-8050-2570-7 (alk. paper)
    1. Gun control—United States—Juvenile literature. I. Title. II. Series.
HV7436.092   1993
363.3'3'0973—dc20
                                              92-34635
                                                  CIP
                                                      AC

Contents

· · · · ·

Introduction

■ ■ ■ ■ ■ ■

The Right to Bear Arms

"A well regulated Militia, being necessary to the security of a free State, the right of the people to keep and bear Arms, shall not be infringed."

—Second Amendment to the U.S. Constitution

Of the first 10 amendments to the Constitution, known as the Bill of Rights, perhaps none is more controversial than the Second Amendment—the amendment that gives every American the fundamental right to bear arms. In 1791, when the amendment became law, our young nation had no standing army, and every able-bodied man was expected to rise to the defense of his country. Americans live in a very different country today. Many people say there are no external threats to our borders that justify guns in the hands of private citizens. The country has a sophisticated defense system, and the only "militia" left is the well-armed National Guard.

Does this mean that the Second Amendment is not relevant to twentieth-century America? Those who favor the use of guns say no. According to them, the Second Amendment grants every law-abiding citizen of the United States the right to own a gun for protection as well as simple peace of mind. To deny that right, they claim, strikes at the very heart of our democracy.

On the other side of the issue are the anti-gun people, who clamor for stricter gun control. They do not see any relationship between our young, untamed, thinly populated republic and the complex, crowded nation that we live in today. They take the position that the easy availability of guns has only served to encourage criminals, increase violent crime, and put guns in the hands of adults and children who misuse them with often deadly results. Make guns difficult to obtain, say the anti-gun people, and we will reduce crime, homicides, and tragic shooting accidents.

The battle over gun control is as heated as the violence in America's streets. It is a debate that no American can afford to ignore, because violence and crime concern all citizens and affect the stability of the nation. This book will attempt to fairly present both sides of the gun-control debate. Coming to a conclusion about this issue is left to the reader. Is the right to bear arms a fundamental liberty worth fighting for, or has it merely become a license to kill? You be the judge.

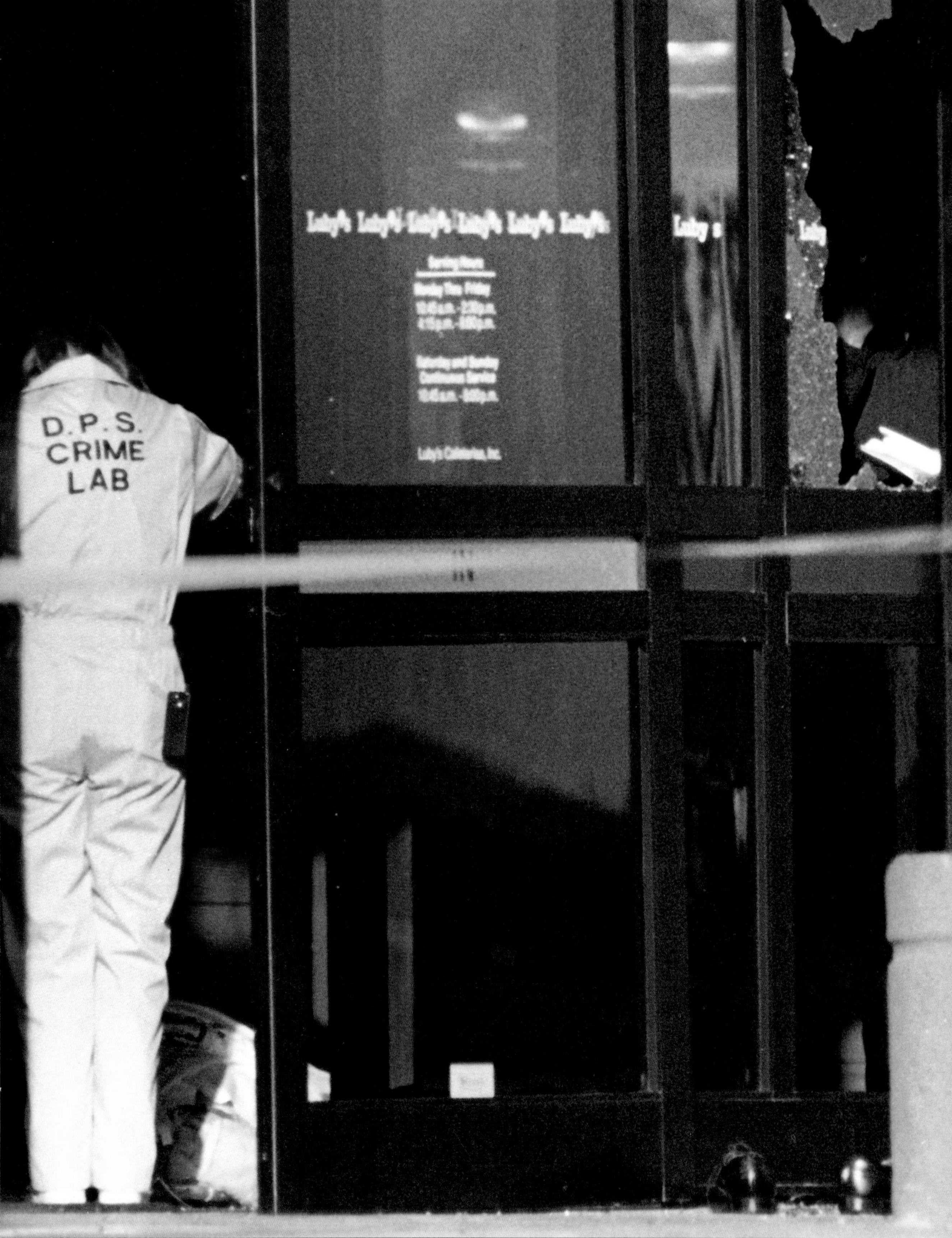
D.P.S.
CRIME
LAB

1

......

Guns in Our Lives

It was just another busy lunchtime at Luby's Cafeteria in the small Texas city of Killeen, about 175 miles north of Houston. The date was October 16, 1991. Suddenly the noontime bustle was interrupted by the terrible sound of shattering glass.

A blue Ford pickup crashed through the restaurant's window. The driver emerged from the vehicle brandishing two semiautomatic pistols. He immediately began firing into the crowd. For 10 minutes he shot people cowering under and behind tables at point-blank range, pausing only to reload his weapons. Finally, four police officers arrived and seriously wounded the mad gunman. He retreated to

Investigators search the wreckage at Luby's Cafeteria in Killeen, Texas, the site of the worst mass murder in U.S. history.

the back of the restaurant and shot himself in the head. When it was over, 23 men and women lay dead—the worst mass murder in U.S. history.

The dead killer was identified as George Hennard, 35, an out-of-work seaman who lived alone in his mother's spacious home in a nearby town. To this day, no one knows what motivated Hennard to go on that bloody rampage.

One of the guns he used was a 9-mm Glock 17, a plastic-framed, rapid-fire pistol he had bought in Nevada. The gun was purchased legally and registered with the Las Vegas police. A reporter for *Time* magazine went out the day after the killings and bought the very same weapon in a nearby discount store. It took her all of 40 minutes.

The day after the killings in Killeen, the House of Representatives voted on a bill that would have banned 13 different assault weapons like the one Hennard had used. Despite the events of the previous day, the measure was voted down 247 to 177.

The tragedy in Killeen, Texas, is just one of many mass killings that have plagued the nation in the twentieth century. These killings have fueled the fiery debate over gun control in America, which has become one of the most controversial issues of our time. The issue also relates to other troubling aspects of modern life, including increased crime, increased drug use, poverty, and urban unrest.

The Gun

Epidemic Mass murders are only the most dramatic illustration of the deadly relationship between guns and crime in America. Handguns are used in more than 600,000 crimes each year, including robberies, homicides, muggings, and rapes. Semiautomatic weapons, such as the ones George Hennard used, are among the weapons of choice for most drug lords and their gang members. They are the weapons capable of creating the most destruction in the least amount of time.

But guns are not just in the hands of criminals and the police. It is estimated that there are some 202 million firearms in the United States and that about half of American families own at least one gun.

Why do all these Americans, many of whom are law-abiding citizens, own guns? Hunting and other shooting sports account for a large percentage of the 40 million rifles owned by Americans. But few of the many more millions of handguns in this country are used for hunting. Easily concealed and most effective at short range, handguns have been the long-standing weapons of criminals.

As crime has risen in the United States, so have the fears of the American people. Over the past two decades, more and more Americans have been buying handguns to protect themselves, their families, their homes and property, and their businesses.

It has become the norm—not the exception—for an inner-city storekeeper to have a gun behind the counter. Women in record numbers are packing lightweight pistols in their purses to deter muggers. High school students add a gun to their book bags to defend themselves from escalating violence in the public schools. Business is booming at target and shooting ranges in all regions of the country, where new gun owners hone their shooting skills. You can even buy a video to help you select the "right" gun and instruct you how to use it. America, it seems, has truly gone gun crazy.

Gun Restrictions

With every freedom granted by our government comes the responsibility to use that freedom wisely. For example, though the First Amendment guarantees free speech, it does not sanction someone shouting "fire" just for the fun of it. Every freedom has its limits. So what are the limits on the right to bear arms? What controls are there on those who can or cannot own a gun?

There are about 20,000 laws restricting the use and sale of firearms on the federal, state, and local levels. Not everyone can own a gun. If you are a known alcoholic, drug addict, or criminal or if you have a documented mental problem, you cannot purchase a gun. Of course, this law is difficult to

Opposite:
Semiautomatic weapons are easily available in the United States and are the preferred weapons of many drug gangs.

Bernhard Goetz and the Question of Vigilante Justice

Bernhard Goetz was just another ordinary face in the crowd of more than 7 million New Yorkers. Following a fateful encounter on a subway one December night in 1984, Goetz became one of the most admired people and,

Bernhard Goetz speaks to the media during his trial in 1985.

at the same time, one of the most despised people in the United States.

Approached by a group of youths on the subway, Goetz believed he was about to be mugged. He pulled out a concealed and unlicensed handgun and shot four of the youths, leaving one permanently paralyzed. Goetz immediately fled to Concord, New Hampshire, where he turned himself in nine days later.

The subway incident set off a nationwide debate about whether what Goetz had done was wrong. Many people called Goetz a hero and applauded him for defending himself. Others were disturbed that without violent provocation someone could shoot four people and then just walk away. The jurors in Goetz's trial were sympathetic; they acquitted him. They were sending out a message that people in urban neighborhoods were tired of being passive victims for criminals and that citizens were ready to fight back. For many Americans who had been victims of violent crimes, or fearful of such crime, the Goetz verdict was a strike back at the criminals. It was a concrete incident in which some kind of "justice" had apparently prevailed. But a more disturbing question remained: Do citizens have the right to take "justice" into their own hands? Should vigilante justice replace due process of law in settling violent crimes? Though the satisfaction of revenge appeals to many people, what would our society be like if each citizen had such power?

enforce. Anyone who buys a weapon must fill out a form that requires a certain amount of background information. But there is nothing to stop a person from lying. Also, most dangerous criminals don't get their guns from legitimate sources, but rather on the black market.

Some communities keep a close watch on every gun that is bought. The buyer is required by law to purchase a license to own a gun and then register its serial number with the local police. In certain communities there is a waiting period, during which police can run a background check on the potential gun buyer. Americans who oppose such measures claim they only hamper the law-abiding citizen and not the criminal, who simply circumvents the law anyway.

There are other restrictions that are more widely accepted. For instance, plastic guns, the latest in weapon technology, cannot be picked up by the metal detectors at airports and other places where security is of utmost importance. Such weapons are a terrorist's dream and have been legally banned from the United States. Then there are the Teflon-coated bullets that can penetrate the bullet-proof vests worn by many police officers who work in high-crime areas. These aptly named "cop-killer bullets" have also been outlawed, as have automatic weapons imported into the United States.

Deadly Force:
Semiautomatic and Automatic Weapons

AK-47, MAC-10, AR-15. These may be meaningless letters and numbers to many people, but to those who know their guns, they all spell one thing—deadly force. They are just three of the arsenal of semiautomatic weapons that have turned the streets and neighborhoods of urban America into armed camps.

While most conventional handguns fire only six bullets before they have to be reloaded, semis can fire hundreds of rounds without being reloaded. Drug gangs have found this superior firepower effective for wiping out competition in their territories or for fighting the police. Drug gangs have also helped make semiautomatic weapons popular with the common criminal and the psychopath, like George Hennard. In order to avoid being outgunned by criminals, police officers and other law-enforcement agents have turned to using some semiautomatic guns, such as miniature submachine guns.

But automatic weapons are even more efficient than semis. Unlike semis, which require a squeeze of the trigger to fire each round, they require only one squeeze to fire hundreds of rounds of ammunition. One automatic rifle can fire up to 900 rounds a minute. Although these weapons are illegal in the United States, many criminals have easily converted their semis into automatics. All it takes in some cases is inserting a matchstick into the gun.

Semiautomatic weapons can fire hundreds of rounds without being reloaded.

These restrictions notwithstanding, guns are still largely unregulated in America today. No gun law stopped George Hennard from getting his hands on two deadly assault weapons, and they probably won't stop the next mass killer either.

America, one of the most powerful nations on earth, is also one of the most violent. Unlike many less fortunate nations, we have no revolution going on, no civil war raging in our country. Our government is stable and democratic, and our society is, overall, affluent compared with most. Yet people are dying every day in our streets, and in alarming numbers. America's murder rate is the highest in the world. More Americans have died from being shot with privately owned guns since 1900 than have died in all the wars that our country has ever fought. This shooting is not wholly related to drug gangs and robberies. Much of the shooting is among people who know each other. Many of the murders are committed during arguments and other confrontations where the anger can easily escalate to a level of deadly violence. How did we get to this alarming point in our society? Are Americans just more likely to settle their arguments with guns than with words or fists? Have guns and killing become an ingrained part of our culture? Many of the answers to these questions, as with most contemporary problems, lie in our country's past.

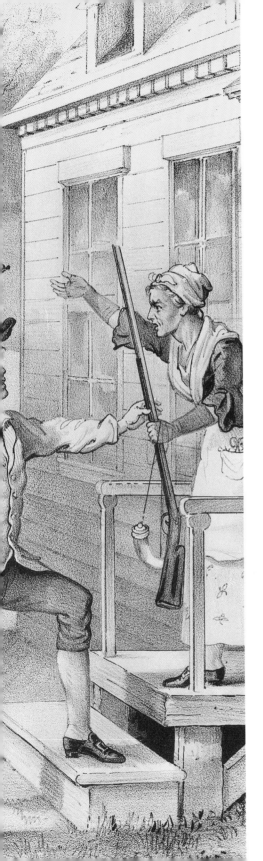

2

......

Is America a Gun Culture?

The scene is a dusty, deserted street in the old West. Two armed men at opposite ends of the street step off a wooden sidewalk and eye each other warily. They begin to walk slowly toward each other. Then they stop, draw their six guns, and fire. One of the men falls dead. The other sticks his still-smoking gun back into its holster and strides away.

This is the classic western showdown, one that is enshrined in a thousand western movies and television shows. Of course, it rarely ever happened that way. Most grudges in the old West were settled in a dark alley with a shot in the back. But that hardly matters. It is the myth, not the harsher reality, that Americans

During the American Revolution, the minutemen needed to be armed at a moment's notice in order to defend the country.

remember. And myth is what has shaped both the beliefs and the opinions that are held today about guns and violence.

Guns in Our History

Guns have played a major role in our nation's history from its very beginning. The earliest European explorers used their firepower to subdue Native Americans who felt threatened by the arrival of strangers. Early settlers were never far from their long rifles, which not only protected them from the Indians, but also provided the means by which to hunt fresh game for food.

No symbol of the Revolutionary War is more sacred to most Americans than the minuteman, the ordinary citizen who answered his country's call at a moment's notice and went off with his rifle to defend America against the British. But again, myth has overrun reality. As historian Richard Hofstadter has pointed out, amateur militiamen, while important early in the Revolution, were quickly replaced by the better-trained professional soldiers of the Continental Army. Commander in chief George Washington held a low opinion of civilians in arms, and it was the army, not the local militia, that turned the tide and won the war.

During the 1800s, guns continued to play a crucial role in America's western expansion. They gave

Opposite:
Billy the Kid was one of the Wild West's most famous and violent outlaws. Today he is romanticized as a symbol of America's frontier past. This is the only known photo of Billy the Kid.

The Bad Guy as Good Guy:
From Jesse James to John Gotti

They call him "the Dapper Don" because he is always immaculately groomed, even while standing trial for murder. John Gotti is the chieftain of one of the nation's largest and most powerful crime families. He remains a figure of mystery and glamour to many Americans, despite his conviction and sentencing to life in prison. Gotti's popularity puts him in the company of celebrated American outlaws stretching back to Jesse James.

America has always had a soft spot for "bad guys." These lawless individuals have frequently been depicted as rebels with a romantic past—rugged men whose exciting lives were usually cut short by the very violence they lived by. America's soft spot for western outlaws was later transferred to the urban gangsters of America's mean streets in the 1920s and 1930s. Gangsters such as John Dillinger and Bonnie and Clyde were glamorized in Hollywood films of the 1960s and were seen as almost tragic heroes by a new generation of Americans. For all the folklore trimmings, these criminals, like many of their western ancestors, were coldhearted killers who turned to crime for profit.

Although America's bad guys have been portrayed more negatively in recent movies, a contradictory attitude nonetheless exists. *Goodfellas*, for example, which is based on the life of a member of the Mafia who turned informer, shows that beneath all the glamour, gangsters are an ugly lot motivated not by loyalty or honor but by greed and vengeance.

And *Bugsy* depicts Bugsy Siegel as a mentally deranged killer but still attempts to make him a romantic and sympathetic hero. The myth of the good "bad guy" thus lives on.

John Gotti was the head of one of America's most powerful crime families. Even when he was on trial for murder and corruption, many Americans called for his acquittal.

men such as trailblazer Daniel Boone, with his Kentucky long rifle, and cowboys and gunslingers, with their Colt revolvers, the courage to venture into unknown territories. Just how wild the Wild West really was is a matter that is debated among historians. The period of widespread lawlessness was relatively short. Towns grew fast, and peace officers were hired to enforce the law. The actual homicide rate per capita in the heyday of legendary towns like Dodge City in Kansas and Tombstone in Arizona, was surprisingly low when compared with the murder rates in today's urban areas.

Violence in the Media

The frontier is long gone in America, but its mythic power continues to hold a fascination for many Americans. Much of this attraction comes from movies and television. They have replaced the dime novels and the cheap paperbacks that first celebrated the exploits, largely fictional, of such real-life figures as Billy the Kid and Buffalo Bill Cody. Today's cop shows and action movies depict violence with weapons far more lethal than Billy the Kid ever could have imagined.

For decades, sociologists have been studying the effect of television and movie violence on viewers. The results are disturbing. In scientific tests, brutal violence has been shown to desensitize adults to a

"Make My Day": All in a Day's Work for Dirty Harry and Company

The Terminator, the sci-fi action picture that made Arnold Schwarzenegger a megastar, contains a memorable scene in which the title character walks into a gun store. The cheerful store clerk sells him a deadly assault rifle and ammo and then watches uneasily as the robotlike customer loads the weapon. The shop owner starts to mildly object as the Terminator turns the gun on him and fires. While the film is pure fantasy, the ease with which the assassin gets his weapon is not very far from reality.

Arnold Schwarzenegger in *The Terminator*.

victim's plight because viewers tend to identify with the person committing the violent act. Much of the violence that Americans see in the entertainment media is frequently casual, quick, and without emotion, with no immediate consequences for the aggressor. In action movies, guns are usually the *first*, not the *last*, resort to solve a problem or settle a conflict. This casual acceptance of violence has had an enormous effect on Americans, especially the young, some of whom believe the best way to settle an argument or even a score is to pull out a loaded gun and fire away.

The Terminator is a fantasy villain, but many of Hollywood's gun-toting stars, like Rambo, Dirty Harry, John McClane of *Die Hard*, and their imitators, are "good guys" who have become cultural heroes to Americans. They are admired not for their intelligence or their social skills, but for their ability to dispatch their enemies with a maximum of deadly force.

What is perhaps most intriguing about these characters is that they usually operate alone and outside the law. Like the lone gunman who "cleaned up the town" in old westerns, these characters fight crime and wrongdoers single-handedly, usually outside the normal system of law and order. Rambo is a one-man war machine, taking on the Vietcong to free prisoners of war. Dirty Harry turns in his police badge when his own department doesn't back up his unconventional methods of catching serial killers. The hero of the popular *Death Wish* films is a vengeful vigilante who preys on muggers and killers by offering himself as a lure in New York City's dark corners. In the *Die Hard* movies, good guy John McClane skillfully uses sophisticated weapons to create great destruction and to exterminate his enemies.

What effect do these fictional characters have on real life? An incident in New York City may provide part of the answer. When a stockbroker was shot on a city street by a 12-year-old boy, the victim watched the youth blow smoke from his revolver, Dirty Harry-style, before riding off on his bicycle. Is this life imitating art or art reflecting life? Many people think that it is becoming increasingly difficult to tell the difference.

A Mix Of Yesterday And Today

Does our frontier past, distorted and magnified by today's media, account for the widespread use of guns and violence in America? It may be part of the answer, but it is not the whole answer. As historian Hofstadter points out, both Canada and Australia share America's frontier past, but they have many strict gun-control laws and relatively low gun-related murder and suicide rates. If these countries have been able to overcome a violent and dangerous past, why hasn't the United States been able to do likewise?

An Era of Assassinations and Mass Murders

To many Americans it is a sad irony that President John F. Kennedy was a member of the NRA (National Rifle Association). In November of 1963, the president was assassinated in Dallas, Texas. In the wake of the tragedy, however, there was no major outcry for gun-control legislation. Five years later, civil rights leader Martin Luther King, Jr., and presidential candidate Robert F. Kennedy were gunned down only months apart. The public

James Earl Ray assassinated Martin Luther King, Jr., in 1968.

outcry at that time was so great that Congress passed the first major piece of national gun-control legislation ever.

The Gun Control Act of 1968 prohibited criminals, minors, the mentally ill, illegal aliens, and drug addicts from buying handguns. It did not satisfy pro-gun or anti-gun-control advocates. The pro-forces felt that the law was useless without a required waiting period or background check. The NRA, on the other hand, believed law-abiding citizens were being inconvenienced by the law for no good reason.

The 1970s and 1980s saw more assassinations and attempted assassinations of public figures. These included an attempt on the life of Alabama governor George Wallace, two attempts on the life of President Gerald Ford in the mid-1970s, the murder of musician John Lennon outside his New York City apartment in 1980, and the attempt on the life of President Reagan the following year.

Increases in the number of assault weapons in recent years have led to highly destructive mass killings. One of the most infamous of these incidents took place in a schoolyard in Stockton, California, in 1988. Five schoolchildren between the ages of six and nine were killed, and 30 others were wounded by an alcoholic drifter named Patrick Purdy. He had used a Chinese-made AK-47 assault rifle. And just a few years later, in October of 1991, the country's worst mass murder, discussed in Chapter 1, took place in Killeen, Texas.

Part of the problem may lie more with America's founders than with our violent frontier past. Many of them, despite George Washington's beliefs, opposed the idea of a "standing army," which they viewed as a symbol of old-time British tyranny. The Founders believed that a militia of ordinary citizens who would defend their country in time of war was better suited to a country based on the principles of freedom and individual liberty.

The feelings that were expressed by our nation's Founders explain the enactment of both the Second Amendment, with its "right to bear arms," and the Third Amendment, which forbids soldiers from taking up residence in the homes of citizens without their consent. Although the American people have long since accepted the necessity of a "standing army" to defend the United States against aggressors, for many citizens the right to possess firearms for defense has become woven into the very fabric of our democracy.

Some experts fail to see any connection between contemporary America's gun culture and our violent past. They see the rise in the use of handguns as a direct result of the growing crime and violence in America's cities and towns. Whatever the connection, it seems that violence is as much a part of American society today as it was in the days of George Washington or Wild Bill Hickok.

3

Kids and Guns

Young people line up at a steel-plated door for their weekly ritual. A grim-faced man, flanked by security guards, beckons them forward one by one. He then runs a metal detector over the perimeter of their bodies and motions them to move on. The search for guns is completed without incident, but worry is far from over for the authorities. Guns have been smuggled in through windows and side doors before. There will be an unannounced shakedown of lockers later in the week.

No, this isn't a house of correction. It's a public high school in a large American city. Why have America's schools been transformed into maximum-security institutions? One

Gun possession among teens and preteens rose steadily in the late 1980s and the early 1990s. In 1992, approximately 45 percent of teens said they either owned a gun or had a friend who did.

reason is that Americans are fascinated by guns, and this fascination has filtered down with alarming speed to the youth of our nation. And nowhere are kids with guns causing more trouble than in the nation's schools.

Guns in Schools

America's schools used to be places where city youths could feel safe and protected even if they were abused at home or victimized in the streets. Not anymore. According to the latest government statistics, nearly 3 million crimes occur each year on or close to school property. That's 16,000 crimes per school day, or 1 crime every six seconds.

According to a survey from the U.S. Bureau of Justice, more than 400,000 students aged 12 to 19 claimed they were victims of violent crime. One survey of high school students in Baltimore showed that out of nearly 400 students, 64 percent knew someone who had carried a handgun to school within the past six months, while 60 percent knew someone who had been robbed, threatened, or shot by a student with a gun.

Why are kids bringing guns to school? And why are they killing each other with them? The answer is more complicated than saying that guns are too easy to get. Violence among youth is a complex

Opposite:
Many schools in America use metal detectors to search students for weapons.

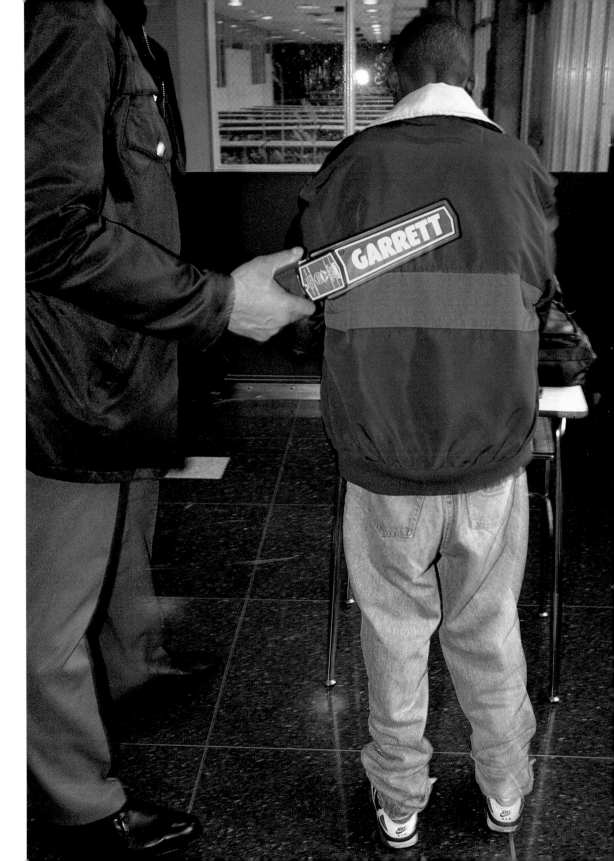

Violence in Schools

Although school violence is on the rise all across America, it is particularly acute in city schools. For New York City, 1991–1992 was the bloodiest school year in history. By March of 1992, there had already been a record 56 shooting incidents in and around schools. The following is a list of some of those incidents.

- **October 7, 1991: Brooklyn**
  A parent is shot in the back by a pellet gun.

- **October 8, 1991: the Bronx**
  A 17-year-old student is shot and killed.

- **October 8, 1991: the Bronx**
  A 14-year-old student is shot in the stomach.

- **October 29, 1991: the Bronx**
  A student is shot in the legs.

- **November 11, 1991: Brooklyn**
  A 19-year-old student is shot in the back by a gang of armed intruders in the school hallway.

- **November 19, 1991: Brooklyn**
  A teacher is shot in the left arm on the street outside school.

- **November 21, 1991: Staten Island**
  A student shoots three other students, killing one 18-year-old.

- **November 25, 1991: Brooklyn**
  A 16-year-old student is killed, and a teacher is wounded in the school hallway.

- **January 21, 1992: Brooklyn**
  A police officer is shot on the street by a student.

- **January 30, 1992: Brooklyn**
  A 13-year-old student and an 11-year-old student are wounded when another student fires shots into a school playground.

Source: United Federation of Teachers: *Newsweek*, March 9, 1992.

social problem caused by many factors. Some kids, especially those involved in drug dealing, bring guns to school just to commit crimes. But there are many more students who, like their parents, carry a gun for defense and self-protection. "You gotta be prepared," says one armed Baltimore junior high school student. "People shoot you for your coat, your rings, chains, anything."

Are Classrooms Doomed to Be Battle Zones?

Thomas Jefferson High School in Brooklyn, New York, is not a typical inner-city school. In the 1990–1991 school year, 81 percent of its mostly black and Hispanic students applied to college. Its principal was awarded a Reader's Digest American Heroes in Education Award. But that didn't stop a double murder from being committed in the school's halls in March of 1992.

Khalil Sumpter, a 15-year-old, pulled out a .38-caliber Smith and Wesson as Tyrone Sinkler and his friend Ian Moore stepped out of a first-period class. Sinkler had served time for a mugging that Sumpter had also been involved in. He accused Sumpter of ratting on him, so he threatened revenge. Without a word, he opened fire on the two youths. Moore, shot through the heart, died instantly. Sinkler died from a head wound within hours. Jefferson High hasn't been the same since.

Like one fourth of the nation's urban school districts, Jefferson High uses metal detectors, locker shakedowns, and armed police patrols to discourage students from carrying guns to school. But the weapons still turn up, often smuggled in through windows or back doors.

What is the answer? How does America prevent its schools from becoming killing grounds? In Chicago public schools, a SAFE (Schools Are for Education) program seems to be working. It relies on random metal-detector checks and unarmed security forces that work closely with city police to root out troublemakers and defuse confrontations. Since the program was started, not one shooting has occurred during school hours.

Programs like SAFE deal with existing problems only; they don't prevent future ones. For long-range solutions, experts say that education is the key. Parents and teachers need to work together to teach kids how to deal nonviolently with conflict. Kids must also be taught the real dangers of guns along with proper procedures for gun safety. Adults need to supervise students, especially at after-school functions, such as sporting events, where violence frequently erupts. Finally, parents need to keep guns empty and locked away, where kids can't get at them.

Students from Brooklyn's Jefferson High School protest school violence.

These are normal, everyday kids. "Good" kids. But that doesn't prevent them from killing one another. Teenagers are less likely than adults to know or respect the lethal power of a loaded gun. The violence they see on television and in the movies has desensitized many of them to the consequences of brutality. So has the real-life violence they see regularly on the urban streets. For many of these youths a gun is a symbol of power, something threatening that can make a "weakling" the equal of a "bully."

"A gun can give someone a sense of power and a security blanket," says a Houston youth psychologist. "They haven't really thought out what they're going to do with it until something happens. But then it's too late."

Senseless

Tragedies The "something" that may provoke the use of a gun can be as trivial as one person stepping on another's shoes, making an insulting remark, or offending someone's girlfriend. In De Kalb, Missouri, a 12-year-old boy brought a .45 semiautomatic to school to take revenge on a classmate who had teased him for being fat. A 13-year-old who was protecting the intended victim was shot instead. The boy with the gun, overcome with emotion, then shot himself in the head.

Opposite:
Parents, teachers, and New York City community leaders mourn victims of school violence in 1992.

De Kalb is not a big, crime-ridden city. But guns are turning up in the hands of many students in far smaller, rural communities across America. In the tiny town of Crosby, Texas, the captain of the football team was shot dead by a 15-year-old girl with a .38-caliber revolver while he was waiting on line in the cafeteria. The reason for the shooting? The boy had allegedly called the girl a bitch.

Where do these guns come from? Some young people buy them on the street for as little as $25. Some steal them. But according to police records, 80 to 90 percent of guns brought to school come from home. In some states, such as California, laws recently have been passed to make parents criminally responsible when their child shoots someone with a gun belonging to the parents.

Guns kept at home don't have to be brought to school to cause tragedy. They can fall into the hands of even younger children with often lethal results. In many cases, a young child wanders into the parents' bedroom, comes across a loaded handgun, and thinks it's a toy. The child then points it at himself or herself, a sibling, or a playmate and pulls the trigger. In one five-year period ending in 1983, more than 88 deaths were reported in California alone from such accidental shootings in which both the shooter and the victim were 14 years old or younger.

Teen

Suicide In addition to the large numbers of young people shooting one another, a rising number of young people are shooting *themselves*. Teen suicide has reached crisis proportions in America, and the problem is only heightened by the easy availability of guns. Adolescents often find themselves on an emotional roller coaster, up one minute and down the next. Some teens become so depressed that they consider suicide. A gun, which offers a quick and

---

Kids with Guns: Facts at a Glance

By the late 1980s and early 1990s, violence in schools and at home had increased dramatically. By 1992, it was not uncommon to find fourth and fifth graders armed with guns in school. "You think it's a bunch of bad kids who are carrying the guns, but it's not," reported a Texas educational health director. "The kids are victims of violence, and the schools are not creating safe environments. Law enforcement is not adequately involved." Here are some statistics about guns in schools:

- According to the Center for Disease Control, 1 student in 5 reports carrying a weapon of some type, and 1 student in 20 (about 5 percent) reports carrying a gun.

- Between 1970 and 1990, the number of young Americans killed by firearms each year more than doubled, from 1,059 to 2,162.

- By 1992, homicide was the leading cause of death for black males under the age of 35.

- In 1991, an estimated 45 percent of teenagers either owned guns themselves or had friends who owned guns.

- An estimated 80 to 90 percent of gun-toting kids get their firearms at home.

- According to the National Crime Survey, almost 3 million crimes occur on or near school campuses each year. That is 16,000 crimes per school day, or 1 crime every six seconds.

- One fourth of major urban school districts were using metal detectors in schools by 1992.

- In California, during the 1988–1989 school year, armed assaults were up 25 percent, for a total of 1,830.

Source: Ronald D. Stephens, National School Safety Center: *Newsweek* magazine, March 9, 1992

irreversible solution to life's problems, can be the most dangerous weapon for a person who is confused and inclined to do things without thinking. In the late 1980s, suicides among kids ages 10 to 14 doubled. In more than half of these deaths a gun was used.

Many psychologists believe that the majority of people who attempt suicide do not really want to die. The attempt, especially in the case of a young person, is frequently a cry for help or attention. The chance of surviving a suicide attempt in which drugs are involved or a knife is used is greater than if a gun is used. A bullet in the head is usually fatal. Statistics have shown that a much higher percentage of males kill themselves with guns than do females. Psychologists believe that men and boys are more comfortable with a quick and final death, even though using a gun is the most violent method.

Regardless of where a person stands on the issue of gun control, responsible adults are in agreement that handguns should be kept empty and out of the reach of young people. The mother of a Detroit boy who was killed as a result of gunplay is a leader in the SOSAD (Save Our Sons and Daughters) movement. According to this parent, we're losing a whole generation of children because of youthful violence.

Opposite:
Boys and men are more likely to use a gun to commit suicide than are girls and women.

4

To Arm or Not to Arm: Both Sides of the Issue

The issue of gun control has bitterly divided America for decades. Advocates both for and against gun restrictions have come up with strong arguments for their side. Americans who are opposed to gun control have, until recently, been more organized and vocal than gun-control groups. Of these anti-gun-control groups, none has been more effective than the National Rifle Association.

The NRA was formed in 1871 by a group of Civil War veterans who were concerned with the poor shooting skills of many of their comrades in the Union Army. Their original purpose was to promote gun safety and good marksmanship among hunters and sportsmen.

Many Americans oppose strict gun-control legislation on the grounds that they have a constitutional right to bear arms.

Members of the NRA have included several presidents—Teddy Roosevelt, who was an avid hunter and conservationist; Eisenhower; Kennedy; Nixon; Reagan; and Bush.

The rapid rise of crime and violence in American cities and towns during the 1960s contributed to the rise of gun-control advocates. In response, the NRA also began to change. It went from being mainly an educational organization to being a political advocate. To prevent gun-control legislation that would stop or hamper people from buying guns, the organization mounted an aggressive membership drive and tripled its membership in only a decade. The money that new membership brought into the NRA was used to lobby Congress to vote down all gun-control legislation.

The Arguments
Against Gun Control
Why are the members of the NRA and millions of other Americans so strongly opposed to gun control? The cornerstone of their opposition is mostly related to the text of the Second Amendment of the Constitution, which declares: "A well regulated Militia, being necessary to the security of a free State, the right of the people to keep and bear Arms, shall not be infringed." In relating this to the maintenance of a state militia, the Second Amendment protects the right as a

collective principle for each of the states. The intention of the framers of the Constitution in drafting this amendment has been a matter of some debate. Historically, however, the Supreme Court has held that the amendment neither guarantees nor implies the right of individuals to own or to carry arms for individual purposes. The Court has also ruled that the Second Amendment does not deny to the states the power to pass laws regulating the ownership or carrying of arms.

As was noted earlier, anti-gun-control advocates fervently believe in the right of every law-abiding citizen to "keep and bear arms." They see this right

Fearing for their safety, increasing numbers of Americans—including women—are buying handguns and learning how to shoot.

as a basic part of our democratic system. They also argue that restrictive laws that are meant to deter crime are doomed to failure. Strict gun laws, they say, affect law-abiding citizens only, not the criminals who obtain their weapons illegally.

By the same token, pro-gun groups claim that making it harder for ordinary citizens to obtain guns will just place them in a more vulnerable position when confronted by well-armed criminals. They point to many cases where store owners have shot or driven off would-be robbers in self-defense. In addition, they cite instances where women have deterred rapists and muggers with a loaded gun. Why, gun supporters ask, should we make innocent citizens even more defenseless against the widespread crime in our nation?

Pro-gun supporters also point to polls that say hardened criminals are more fearful of a civilian with a gun than a police officer. This is for good reason. According to one Justice Department report, armed citizens annually kill two to three times the number of criminals than are killed by police officers.

The NRA in particular uses the "domino theory" to support its opposition to even the mildest form of gun control. If we give in "an inch," this argument asserts, the opposition will end up taking "a mile." "If we give in on the handgun waiting period and assault rifles...six months later the anti-gunners

Opposite:
For many law-abiding Americans, guns have several practical uses. Farmers use guns to control pests and protect livestock, and a number of Americans use rifles for sporting purposes.

Guns for Self-Defense

During the Los Angeles riots in the spring of 1992, the only thing that seemed to keep many small businesses from destruction—and their owners from personal injury—was a loaded gun. Korean merchants and other store owners were targeted by rioters who resented their presence in black and Hispanic neighborhoods. When the store owners fired a shot or two over the heads of the looters, the potential criminals immediately looked for another store to loot.

The circumstances of the Los Angeles riots dramatically illustrate one of the strongest arguments of Americans who oppose gun control: Citizens need guns for self-defense. In a nation that is plagued by violent crime, especially in the inner cities, where police protection is often poor, guns are seen as the last hope for survival. The NRA makes a very strong case for citizens—particularly women—arming themselves. The NRA cites incidents such as these:

A 51-year-old Los Angeles, California, woman had been raped by the same man twice. He had not yet been apprehended. After the second assault, she purchased a handgun. The man returned a third time. His criminal career came to an abrupt end.

When authorities in Phoenix, Arizona, responded to an emergency call, they found a 77-year-old woman gently rocking in her favorite chair. Her .38-caliber revolver was pointed at a man who was obediently lying half in and half out of her "pet door."

Until Americans feel that the nation's streets are safe, it seems likely that people who live or work in high-crime areas will continue to buy and carry guns for protection. These same people will most probably vigorously defend the anti-gun-control position.

Many business owners successfully defended their property with guns during the Los Angeles riots in the spring of 1992.

will want our long guns," says past NRA president Jim Reinke.

The NRA insists the solution to the rising tide of crime in America is not stricter gun control but stricter laws, stiffer sentences for violent criminals, more police, and more prisons. Guns, it claims, are not the problem. According to the NRA, people, not guns, kill people.

The Arguments for Gun Control

It almost seems that for every argument *against* gun control there is an argument *for* gun control. Gun-control advocates argue that the Second Amendment gives no license to the general public to own guns, but gives that right only to a well-regulated militia. On this point, they seem to be supported even by the Supreme Court. In 1983, two men who were charged with transporting unlicensed shotguns across state lines claimed their actions were protected by the Second Amendment. The Supreme Court felt otherwise. It ruled that the Second Amendment didn't apply to individuals unless the weapons used served "some reasonable relation to the preservation or efficiency of a well-regulated militia."

As for gun control having no effect on reducing crime, the pro-gun-control lobby contends this just isn't true. If crime rates are any indication, they

say, gun control laws *do* make a major difference. Handgun Control, a gun-control group, reported that in one year deaths by handguns in the United States numbered 8,092, while in Israel they were 18, in Great Britain they were 8, and in Australia, they were 5. All these other countries have strict gun laws. Even within the United States, major crime patterns appear to be directly related to handgun availability. The highest rate of handgun possession in the nation is in the South, which also has the highest murder rate. The annual murder rates are considerably lower in the Northeast and in the north central states, where there are stricter handgun-control laws.

What about the popular pro-gun case for a safe, well-armed citizenry? Gun-control advocates cite statistics and claim there is only a remote chance for a person being attacked to access and use a gun. Assaults just happen too fast. They also point to statistics that indicate armed individuals are more likely to shoot victims who themselves have guns.

Gun-control advocates say that the "guns don't kill people" argument is misleading. If people want to kill people, they can most effectively do it with a gun. Few people lose their lives settling their differences with fists or even baseball bats. With a gun, all it takes is one well-placed bullet. There is no second chance, no time to change your mind.

Opposite:
Law-enforcement officials seize hundreds of thousands of illegal guns each year.

A victim of a drive-by shooting lies dead on a street in Washington, D.C. Gun-control advocates say that much of America's violent crime would be reduced with stricter gun-control measures.

Advocates of gun control say that the "domino theory" put forth by the opposition is a groundless fear. Although there are people who would like to see all guns disappear from our society, most pro-gun-control advocates are concerned mainly about handguns. They say that they have no intention of taking rifles and shotguns away from America's responsible hunters and other sports enthusiasts. Handguns and assault weapons, gun-control forces argue, have no other purpose than to take human life. They want to ban these weapons completely. A forceful argument for banning hand-guns was made by Senator Howard Metzenbaum of Ohio: "We know of only one instance in which [an AK-47 semiautomatic] was used for hunting—when a psychopath in California [Patrick Purdy] went hunting for schoolchildren."

The

Brady Bill
In 1992, while some states had already banned the sale of lethal assault weapons, the fate of the Brady bill—a major piece of national gun-control legislation—remained uncertain. Passed in May of 1991 by the House of Representatives, the Brady bill called for a mandatory seven-day waiting period before a person could complete the legal purchase of a gun. According to Brady bill advocates, the proposed waiting period will have two advantages. First, the local police could run a thorough background check on the potential buyer, making sure the information given on the required form is accurate. Secondly, if a person is buying a gun in an enraged or confused state of mind, the waiting period gives that person time to "cool off" and reconsider the consequences. According to supporters of the Brady bill, this "time-out" could save thousands of lives each year.

Waiting periods have already been shown to be effective. States such as Maryland, California, and New Jersey had a legal waiting period before the Brady bill was passed by the House. In those states, police have identified and arrested thousands of convicted criminals through background checks. They have also successfully prevented those who shouldn't have a gun from legally getting their hands on one.

The Brady Story

The Brady bill is named for a man whose life might be very different today if a gun-control law had existed a decade ago.

James Brady was Ronald Reagan's press secretary in 1981. On March 31 of that year, the newly elected president was leaving a Washington hotel with several people when shots rang out. President Reagan and three of those who were with him were wounded. Reagan recovered, but Brady, who was shot in the head, was left permanently disabled. John Hinckley, the would-be assassin, had bought the gun that he used in a Dallas pawnshop. Hinckley, who had been under psychiatric care, lied on his gun application, and Texas had no waiting period to allow for a police background check on him.

Today, James Brady and his wife, Sarah, are dedicated lobbyists for gun control. After years of being turned down by legislators, the Brady bill was finally passed by the House in 1991. Some gun-control activists see the bill as a milestone. Others see it as only a first step toward getting guns off our streets. Whatever results come from this bill, the debate over gun control is far from over.

Below: Secret Service agents scramble to protect President Reagan and his aides after shots were fired.
Opposite: James Brady after the passage of the Brady bill by the House in May 1991.

5

......

The Future: More Guns or More Control?

What does the future hold for gun control? Based on the present, the outlook is uncertain. On one hand, Americans seem to be in favor of more gun control. On the other hand, they are buying guns in record numbers for protection in an increasingly crime-ridden nation.

The contradictions can best be seen in a state such as California, which is on the cutting edge of gun control. In March 1989, it became the first state to ban assault rifles, prohibiting their sale, manufacture, and possession. At the end of May 1992, following the Los Angeles riots, however, California experienced a 62 percent increase in firearm sales for the year. It seems that the disgust with the violence and death

An illegal shipment of guns that has been impounded sits in an American airport.

caused by guns is very real, as real as the fear of being caught without a gun.

If there is reason for optimism among gun-control advocates in the 1990s, it is largely because of the weakening of the NRA. The once all-powerful NRA lobby has lost much of its grip on Congress, as gun-control advocates have become more vocal and better organized. At the same time, the NRA's rank-and-file membership, which has diminished, has taken a more moderate stance on gun control. According to a 1990 *Time*/CNN poll, 87 percent of gun owners favor a seven-day waiting period for handgun purchases, and 75 percent favor the registration of all semiautomatic weapons and handguns.

In 1988, the NRA lobby lost its first statewide referendum when Maryland refused to repeal a law banning some handguns. In May 1990, New Jersey followed California's lead in banning assault rifles, but it allowed gun owners a year of grace to sell their weapons out of state, remove the firing pin, or turn in the weapons to the police.

Most recently, the NRA has done everything in its power to stop the Brady bill from becoming a law. It has offered an alternative to the seven-day waiting period, calling for a national computer data bank for instant identification of criminals by their fingerprints. Many have found this proposal too impractical and costly.

New York representative Charles E. Schumer is a vocal gun-control leader in Congress. Schumer and other members of Congress will determine the fate of gun control in America.

With the passage of the Brady bill by the House in May 1991, the NRA was dealt a sharp blow. "The stranglehold of the NRA on Congress is now broken," said congressional gun-control leader and New York representative Charles E. Schumer. "They had their aura of invincibility...and they were beaten."

Beaten, but far from defeated, the NRA continues to raise millions of dollars to ensure that gun-control legislation is not passed. It has pledged to continue to be a significant factor for years to come.

Many Americans believe that better law enforcement is the most effective way to control guns. Here, agents from the Bureau of Alcohol, Tobacco, and Firearms display weapons seized from gang members in Los Angeles.

As for the Brady bill, Sarah and Jim Brady see it only as a first step in controlling the sale of guns. Their long-range goal is a comprehensive national list of convicted felons and psychiatric patients that will also be used to screen perspective gun buyers. While it would be much more practical than the NRA's proposal, the Brady plan would still cost 100 million dollars.

Some critics of the Brady plan point out that, while it may limit the legitimate sale of guns, it will do nothing to keep guns out of the hands of the worst criminals. About 83 percent of criminals buy their weapons on the black market. Some gun-control advocates propose an ambitious national registry of every handgun purchase. The registry would supposedly help police officers to trace gun traffickers and then to prosecute them.

A number of gun manufacturers are helping to lessen America's escalating violence. In March of 1989, Colt Manufacturing agreed to suspend sales of civilian copy M-16 rifles, the AR-15, to everyone but the police and the military.

Some gun-control advocates would like to see manufacturers of handguns also improve the safety of their weapons. One suggestion proposes the redesigning of safety catches so they are automatically and permanently engaged unless held in a disengaged position. Another idea is to make guns in such a way that users can easily determine if the weapons are loaded.

Many American gun-control advocates are looking to countries that have stricter gun-control laws as potential models for the United States. Most European countries require handguns to be licensed or registered. In Canada, a citizen must give a good, specific reason to own a handgun; protection is not high on the acceptable list of reasons. Of course, Canada's crime rate is low compared with that of the United States, and there is less reason for a person to need a gun for protection.

Must Americans be prepared to risk their safety and turn in their guns in order to break the vicious cycle of violence and death? Can our country turn

Younger and Younger:
Violent Crime and America's Future

In September 1992, a judge in Pennsylvania sentenced a 13-year-old boy to an 8-year probation for murder. The defendant, Cameron Kocher, was only 9 years old when he shot and killed a 7-year-old girl with whom he was playing. Kocher is believed to be the youngest murder defendant in U.S. history.

It seems that America's violent criminals are getting younger and younger. Between 1985 and 1991, the number of teens arrested on the criminal charge of homicide increased significantly. The biggest increase occurred among 15-year-old boys, whose rate of arrest increased 217 percent from 1985 to 1991, according to a 1992 study from the National Crime Analysis Program at Northeastern University in Boston. The study also reported that the rate of arrest for boys 12 years old and younger increased by 100 percent.

For all young people, male and female alike, the number of arrests for violent crimes increased 27 percent from 1980 to 1990. According to the FBI (Federal Bureau of Investigation), the crime increases span all races, income levels, and backgrounds. In an official statement, it said that a primary reason for this rise in violence was the fact that it was increasingly easy for young people to obtain both drugs and illegal guns.

Lawmakers and citizens had differing opinions about how to best deal with the growing rate of violent crime among America's youth. Many state governors favored plans that would allow young criminals to serve terms in adult prisons. They believed that exposure at an early age to such prisons would deter young criminals from repeating their crimes. Many Americans, however, opposed the idea of punishing youths as adults. According to a poll by the University of Michigan, most adults favored adult prison sentences only for young criminals convicted of murder or rape. Other criminals, they believed, should be reformed through education instead of punishment. Still others said that the only way to reduce the number of crimes committed by young people with guns is to impose stricter regulations on guns. These gun-control advocates believed that, because the majority of young people in America get guns from their homes, the only way to reduce gun-related crimes is to reduce gun access for everyone.

its back on its gun culture in an attempt to save its future and its youth from destruction? Certainly, gun control alone will not end crime and violence. But more and more Americans today believe that some gun control is necessary.

The debate over gun control has been one of the most divisive in American society. It touches on such emotional issues as personal safety, constitutional rights, and the question of how to deal with the violence and crime that threaten our nation.

For many Americans, the idea of restricting the right to bear arms—and, as they believe, the right to properly defend oneself—goes against the very principles upon which this nation was built. Even though America is no longer an untamed frontier, many people say that the nation's urban streets are far more dangerous and lawless than anything that came before. These citizens see guns as essential tools for protection and a means by which each person can assert his or her individual freedoms.

Many Americans, however, believe that a lack of gun control destroys much more than it protects. Those in favor of gun restrictions say that easy access to powerful weapons has turned America into an explosive and highly destructive society. For these Americans, the increase in gun use has created a nation in which personal freedoms and rights are in *greater* danger because many criminals are better armed than the police.

The issues surrounding gun control affect every citizen's life and the workings of the entire nation. Although the answers are not easy, it is certain that Americans must decide these issues in such a way that everyone feels his or her rights are indeed being fairly protected.

Glossary

assault rifle A rapid-fire rifle intended mainly for warfare.

automatic weapon A rifle or handgun that fires hundreds of rounds of ammunition with just one squeeze of the trigger.

Bill of Rights The first 10 amendments to the U.S. Constitution. It guarantees the fundamental rights and freedoms of every citizen.

Brady bill A legislative bill that, if enacted, will require a mandatory seven-day waiting period before a person can conclude the purchase of a gun. This would allow law-enforcement officials to run thorough background checks on buyers.

Gun Control Act of 1968 A federal law that prohibits criminals, minors, the mentally ill, illegal aliens, and drug addicts from purchasing handguns. Each gun buyer must fill out a form, stating if he or she falls into any of these categories.

handgun Any firearm that can be held and fired with one hand, such as a revolver or pistol.

lobbyist A person or group that tries to persuade lawmakers to vote in a particular way on a proposed piece of legislation.

militia A body of civilians called to fight in the armed forces in a time of national emergency. The Militia Act of 1792 called for every "free able-bodied white male citizen" between 18 and 45 to serve in the militia. Today's militia units include the National Guard and the Reserves.

National Rifle Association (NRA) An organization for hunters and sports enthusiasts that promotes gun safety and good marksmanship and is a major lobbyist against gun control.

Second Amendment The amendment to the U.S. Constitution that states: "A well regulated Militia, being necessary to the security of a free State, the right of the people to keep and bear Arms, shall not be infringed." It is the cornerstone of the argument against gun control in the United States.

semiautomatic weapon A rifle or handgun that can fire hundreds of rounds of ammunition without being reloaded. Unlike an automatic weapon, a semi requires the trigger to be squeezed for each round that is fired.

vigilante An individual acting alone or as a member of a self-appointed citizen's group that punishes criminals outside the process of the law.

For Further Reading

Brown, Gene. *Violence on America's Streets.* Brookfield, CT: The Millbrook Press, 1992.

Dolan, Edward F. *Gun Control: A Decision for Americans.* New York: Franklin Watts, 1978.

Landau, Elaine. *Armed America: The Status of Gun Control.* Englewood Cliffs, NJ: Julian Messner, 1991.

Nisbet, Lee, ed. *The Gun Control Debate—You Decide.* Buffalo, NY: Prometheus Books, 1990.

Zimring, Franklin E., and Hawkins, Gordon. *The Citizen's Guide to Gun Control.* New York: Macmillan, 1987.

Source Notes

"A Blow to the NRA." *Time*, May 20, 1991, p. 26.

"Gun Control." *World Book Encyclopedia*, 1987.

Hofstadter, Richard. "America as a Gun Culture." *The Gun Control Debate—You Decide*, ed. by Lee Nisbet. Buffalo, NY: Prometheus Books, 1990.

Kriegel, Leonard. "A Loaded Question." *Harper's*, May 1992, pp. 45–51.

Landau, Elaine. *Armed America: The Status of Gun Control.* Englewood Cliffs, NJ: Julian Messner, 1991.

"National Rifle Association." *World Book Encyclopedia*.

Nordland, Rod. "Deadly Lessons." *Newsweek*, March 9, 1992, pp. 22–30.

"Under Fire." *Time*, January 29, 1990, pp. 16–23.

Wintemute, Garen J. "When Children Shoot Children." *The Gun Control Debate—You Decide*, ed. by Lee Nisbet. Buffalo, NY: Prometheus Books, 1990.

Woodbury, Richard. "Ten Minutes in Hell." *Time*, Oct. 28, 1991, pp. 31–34.

Index

Photo Credits

Cover: Gamma-Liaison; pp. 6–7: ©John Davenport/Gamma-Liaison; p. 10: Gamma-Liaison; p. 12:
AP/Wide World Photos; p. 14: Gamma-Liaison; pp. 16–17: Library of Congress; p. 19: AP/Wide
World Photos; p. 20: Gamma-Liaison; p. 22: AP/Wide World Photos; p. 24: Gamma-Liaison; pp.
26–27: AP/Wide World Photos; p. 29: ©Jon Levy/Gamma-Liaison; p. 31: ©Jon Levy/Gamma-
Liaison; p. 32: ©Jon Levy/Gamma-Liaison; p. 36: Chuck Peterson/©Blackbirch Graphics, Inc.; pp.
38–39: AP/Wide World Photos; p. 41: ©F. Carter Smith/Gamma-Liaison; p. 42: ©Randy G. Taylor/
Gamma-Liaison; p. 44: ©Jean Marc Giboux/Gamma-Liaison; p. 46: AP/Wide World Photos; p. 48:
©Mark Reinstein/Gamma-Liaison; p. 50: Gamma-Liaison; p. 51: ©Terry Ashe/Gamma-Liaison; pp.
52–53: AP/Wide World Photos; p. 55: AP/Wide World Photos; p. 56: AP/Wide World Photos.
Charts by Sandra Burr.